Old LEITH

by

Guthrie Hutton

One of Leith's new 'electric cars' in 1905, just east of the junction of where Hawthornvale and, to the left, Stanley Road meet Newhaven Road. The original tram terminus, beside Belvedere House was at the junction of Stanley Road and Craighall Road.

ISBN 1-872074-65-0

Grain was always one of Leith's principal imports and milling one of the main industries. These jolly millers worked at John Wilson and Co Ltd.'s Swanfield Mill in Bonnington Road, once one of many mills in Leith. The site is now a small industrial estate.

INTRODUCTION

The Burgh of Leith that amalgamated reluctantly with Edinburgh in 1920 stretched from Wardie Burn in the west to Seafield in the east and from the shores of the Forth to Lochend and Pilrig in the south. It contained the industrial port itself, the seaside suburb of Trinity and the ancient fishing village of Newhaven. It had been a separate burgh for only eighty seven years, but in that time had delighted in cocking a snook at its larger neighbour. One of its more spectacular displays of independence was to develop one of the first electric tram systems in Britain in defiance of Edinburgh's attempts to install cable cars throughout the area.

Money for the provision of separate services, however, was always tight and as the nineteenth century wore on a rapidly rising population, attracted by work in industry and the docks, compounded the Council's problems. Overcrowding and poverty became serious, but despite efforts to clear the slums the problems remained. Successive Councils were reluctant to seek salvation in amalgamation and the First World War allowed the decision to be put off, but in 1919 Edinburgh forced the issue. The city sought a boundary extension which would take in Leith and, despite overwhelming rejection by the people of Leith, it went ahead. Leith, Newhaven and Trinity became part of Scotland's capital.

Trinity had developed from a desirable late 18th century location for country villas into a 19th century commuter suburb. Newhaven was an ancient fishing community that was suddenly propelled into prominence when King James IV set up a Royal dockyard there. He expected it to rival Leith as the main port for Scotland; it didn't.

Leith was only a mile and a half from Scotland's capital city and was always strategically and commercially important. Edinburgh's rights as a royal burgh, to use the port for foreign trade, prevented Leith from charging it dues and caused much bitterness; but Leith suffered in other ways too.

After the death of James V, Henry VIII sent an English army north in 1544, to 'persuade' the Scots to agree to the betrothal of the infant Mary to his son Edward. It destroyed Newhaven and Leith, but went home empty handed. Another army put Leith to fire and sword in 1547, but again failed to persuade the Scots. Mary was spirited away to France and in her absence her mother, Mary of Guise, ruled as Regent, supported by French troops. She valued Leith highly and had a palace built in the town, but, fearing the advance of the Reformation, ordered her garrison to fortify the port. For seven months in 1560 Catholic French defenders and Protestant English besiegers slugged it out across the earliest artillery defences in Britain. The siege ended when Mary died; leaving the people of Leith to pick up the pieces of their shattered town and perhaps reflect on the value of the Auld Alliance.

The following year the eighteen year old Mary Queen of Scots arrived at Leith to begin her troubled six year reign.

Since those turbulent years, the port and surrounding communities have been briefly threatened by other military men, but now a new invader is occupying the area. An army of incomers attracted by the bars and restaurants of the Shore and Newhaven Harbour is injecting new life into places depopulated by town planners in the 1950's and 60's. Cruise ships bring flocks of tourists to the Western Harbour. New blocks of flats face the non-tidal, ponded surface of the Water of Leith and along the old dockside the new Scottish Office building is yet another facet of the changing character of Leith.

Guthrie Hutton, May 1995.

FOOT OF LEITH WALK.
(AS IT WAS)

The main road to Leith, in times past, was not Leith Walk, but Easter Road, with another road through Bonnington to the west, which, if it was ever called Wester Road, certainly isn't called that now. The pedestrian 'walk' was apparently formed in the seventeenth century but when the North Bridge and Edinburgh New Town were built, horses and carriages started to use it and quickly turned the surface into ruts and potholes. Queen Victoria's statue, erected at the foot of the Walk in 1907, is still one of Leith's principal landmarks, despite having to be moved to meet the demands of modern traffic, but these buildings, on the corner of Duke Street, were removed completely to make way for the modern traffic of a different age. Leith Central station was built on the site. The lamp on the left is at the start of the Kirkgate.

4

KIRKGATE, LEITH.

The Kirkgate was old Leith's main street. It was narrow, and in the early days made even narrower by projecting stairs and shop signs, and it was not quite straight; a product of the days before town planners. But the planners came in the 1960's and, in one of the worst excesses of that decade, destroyed it. All that remains in the eerie, echoing silence is Trinity House on the left here and South Leith Parish Church opposite. The church started life as St. Mary's Chapel in 1483 and was partly destroyed in the siege of 1560. The ruined remains were taken over by the Reformers, but the church was not completely re-built until 1847; little remains of the original. Even less remains of the Trinity House of 1555 which was replaced by the present building in 1816.

Kirkgate, Leith.

The domestic ordinariness of the other buildings in the Kirkgate was in marked contrast to these grand survivors. In a quintessential old Scots streetscape there were tall tenements cheek by jowl with smaller houses with whitewashed steps and on either side was a warren of closes, vennels, pends and wynds. The Kirkgate was a friendly, pulsating, lively, crowded street, so crowded that policemen couldn't walk down it side by side. Cats basked in the sun on the ledges of dusty windows while human kind bustled in and out of shops: so many and so diverse that some people never shopped anywhere else. There were specialist butchers and penny stores, fish shops and hairdressers; tea and sugar came straight from the sack, broken biscuits from glass topped bins, two ounces of sweets cost a few pence and ... the list is endless!

Pictorial Post Card.

For inland communications only | Address on this side.

Half-penny stamp.

New Gaiety Theatre,
LEITH.

ON MONDAY, FEBRUARY 1st,
For Six Nights at 7-30. (Saturday Night at 7-15).

Monday	Hamlet
Tuesday	Merchant of Venice
Wednesday	Romeo & Juliet
Thursday	Othello
Friday	David Garrick
	Preceded by "Delicate Ground."
Saturday Evening	Macbeth

Mr. IAN MACLAREN as "HENRY V."

The prominent street lamps on the previous page are outside the New Gaiety Theatre, one of two theatres in the Burgh. The Alhambra in Leith Walk was the other. This postcard, issued in 1909, advertised a week of what the local paper described as 'legitimate theatre', presumably to distinguish it from the preceding pantomime; Beauty and the Beast. The paper's critic described the company as '... capable', Mr. MacLaren as '... possessing histrionic talents of no mean degree' and the audiences as '... large and appreciative'. In a clear win for the panto. however, the audiences for Beauty and the Beast '... filled every part of the house' and '... gave the performers a hearty reception'. In the 1950's, Goldilocks appeared on stage with a real bear - Beauty was no doubt relieved they didn't go in for realism in her day!

The Tolbooth of Leith was built in 1565 and administered justice until 1820 when it was demolished. A tenement was built on the site. Tolbooth Wynd, like the Kirkgate, was noted for the variety of its shops. Half way down the left hand side of the Wynd, in this view looking towards the Shore from the Kirkgate, was William Jeffrey and Son, drapers, where generations of Leithers were kitted out. At Christmas time, Santa Claus dispensed glass beads and toy cars from a barrel. The children, clutching their new treasures, then sat spellbound on the floor of an improvised cinema watching cartoon films while their parents did the Christmas shopping in comfort. Jeffrey's supplied the distinctive striped cloth for Newhaven fishwives' dresses too and they also bought their headgear from a Tolbooth Wynd bonnet maker.

Tolboothwynd, Leith.

The local paper, the Leith Observer, had its offices in Tolbooth Wynd; it vigorously opposed the merger with Edinburgh and suggested a poll to canvas Leith opinion, which the Council unwisely took up. Armed with paper's hostility and the Council's indecision, the voters, not surprisingly, rejected amalgamation; by 6 to 1. But, when the battle was over, the paper changed its name to the Edinburgh and Leith Observer: if you can't beat 'em, join 'em! Tolbooth Wynd disappeared with the Kirkgate in the 1960's and no doubt the paper's fiercely pro-Leith editorial line would have condemned their destruction and derided the sterile uniformity of the blocks of flats that replaced them. It was the irregular building line and varied width that gave these old streets such character, even if the buildings had to go, that at least could have been kept.

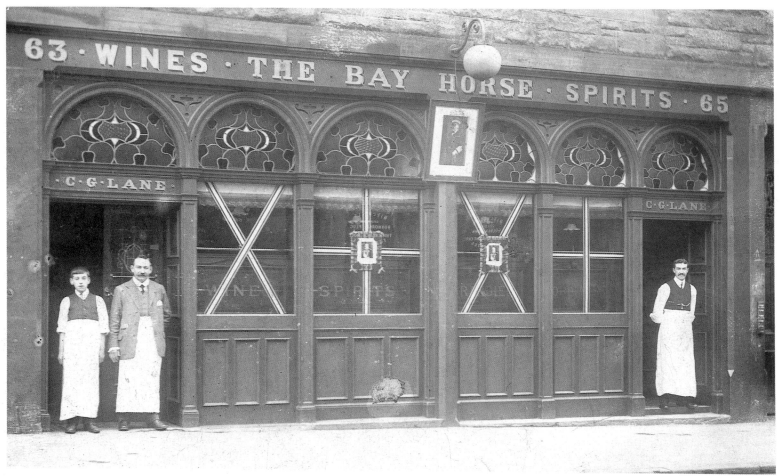

In the 1880's slum dwellings west of the Kirkgate were cleared as part of the Leith Improvement Scheme. New streets with more spacious tenement houses were built to replace them and Henderson Street, named after the then Provost of the Burgh, was one. The Bay Horse pub, in Henderson Street, seen here about 1910, still looks very much as it did when it was built. The area's association with the drinks trade however goes back much further than pub or street, because opposite the Bay Horse is the sixteenth century warehouse and wine cellar known as the Vaults, a survivor of the days when Leith was a centre for importing wine and brandy. Set into the surrounding wall is the Porter's Stone; a replica of a carved stone, originally from Tolbooth Wynd, which shows men shifting barrels.

10

Despite its association with the drinks trade, Leith's history has a sobering capacity to repeat itself rather too often. In the same way that the planners of the 1960's thought they were 'improving' the Kirkgate and Tolbooth Wynd, so the improvers of the 1880's thought they were right to demolish these buildings. Mary of Guise's 'palace' is usually said to have been in Water Street, so this semi-derelict building in Coalhill may not have been her residence, but the newly resurgent Leith would no doubt have been quick to capitalise on such a piece of history if it had not been 'improved'. The mud bank at the corner of the wharf walls shows what the river was like at low tide before the dock gates fixed it at a constant level.

1758. THE SWING BRIDGE. LEITH.

JUDGES

The fifteenth century Brig o' Leith, at the up-stream end of Coal Hill, was replaced in 1787 by this opening bridge, opposite the end of Tolbooth Wynd. It became known as the Upper Drawbridge; another bridge at Bernard Street, built in the mid-1880's, was known as the Lower Drawbridge. The bridges allowed boats to navigate up river as far as Junction Bridge. Here the 260 ton coaster Braeside, of Sunderland, eases her 20 foot beam through the narrow opening to reach one of the upper wharfs. The opening bridge decks have now been removed and replaced by a stone centre arch. In the background is the high steeple of St Thomas' Church, now used as the Guru Nanak Gurdwara Sikh Temple.

12

1757. THE SWING BRIDGE. LEITH.

This picture, and the one on the preceding page, show how slowly and carefully boats went through these bridges (either that or the photographer was in training for the Powderhall sprint). It also appears that the coaster is not operating solely under her own power but is being helped through the bridge, with a line from her bow, presumably to a tug. This kind of lifting bridge is known as a bascule bridge, from the French word meaning see-saw, which aptly describes its action. There were two other opening bridges spanning the Water of Leith. One was a dock railway bridge behind the Custom House and the other was the distinctive Victoria Bridge. It carried pedestrian, road and rail traffic and was the largest swing bridge in Britain when opened in 1874.

13

W. GRAHAM — YOOLL & Cos
WHARF AND WAREHOUSES, LEITH.

There seems to have been no limit to the business interests of W Graham-Yooll & Company. They were oil merchants, drysalters, colour and varnish merchants, cement, whiting and stucco importers, builder's merchants, engineers' furnishers, stone, step, brick and lime merchants - you name it, they did it! Their wharf and warehouses were at the foot of Sheriff Brae beside where the eastern abutment of the old Brig o' Leith had been. The site is now a block of modern flats. It is hard to imagine the scale of shipping and trade that the narrow (and at that time tidal) river between here and Junction Bridge supported. Above Yooll's yard was Hawthorn's engineering works and shipbuilding yard; they built railway engines too. There were other shipyards and coal wharfs on the west bank.

14

A stranger to the Shore, approaching from the west, will briefly see what Leith once was - a bustling seaport with high waterfront buildings crammed together in that wonderfully sculptural way the old Scots builders had of working with rubble stone and wood. But it will only be an initial impression, because a closer look reveals various imitations and some more modern blots on a townscape once filled with gems of Scottish architecture. One survivor is the Kings Wark, one of four tenements built to replace an earlier structure that burned down in 1695. The Stewart monarchs used it as a warehouse, store and residence. They would have been most upset if they could have foreseen the last monarch to arrive at Leith; the Hanoverian George IV. He came ashore in 1822 at a nearby spot now known as the King's Landing.

E.Th. Beruldsen of 47 Shore was a Clothier and Outfitter selling suits, shirts, hosiery, oilskins, sea-boots (Baltic), shoes, slippers, engineers' outfits, boiler suits, etc., and all 'at moderate prices'. The boy in the picture is a Kenneth Scott who sent it in June 1906 to a Mr and Mrs Scott of Kirkwall in Orkney, he was presumably their son. He describes the man as his foreman and hopes his parents like the look of the shop. Such a picture of commercial entrepreneurship could hardly fail to have impressed them, but they may have been less happy with Scott junior's working environment if they had seen the wine and spirit merchants on either side of the shop. A modern block of flats now occupies the site on the corner of the Shore and Broad Wynd.

16

The Shore was once a grubby waterfront where ships lay in the river just across the cobbled street from rough pubs and houses of ill repute. Here the Britannia, a 730 ton coaster of the Leith, Hull and Hamburg Steam Packet Co. appears to be flying a Blue Peter flag to show that she will be leaving on the tide. Behind her, the 17th century round tower was originally a windmill that was later used as a signal tower to let ships arriving at the port know the depth of water at the harbour bar. The building on the extreme left is the Leith Sailor's Home built in 1885 to replace earlier premises in Dock Street. It has now been converted into an up-market hotel and restaurant. The rich fare on offer would be beyond the wildest dreams of the old salts, once just grateful for a bowl of soup in a safe refuge from the sea.

When Queen Victoria came to town in 1842, instead of sailing into Leith as monarchs had done for centuries, she came ashore at Granton. The effect was dramatic, the Leith Dock Commission, which had been set up in 1826, realised that improvements to the inadequate, tidally restricted and badly run port were needed. Victoria Dock was opened in 1851, the harbour improved and the tidal sand bar dredged. The East Pier was extended and a new West Pier built with a railway along it. As trade expanded more new docks were needed. The Albert Dock was added in 1869, followed by the Edinburgh Dock in 1881 and the Imperial Dock in 1903. The Western Harbour was completed in the 1940's and in the 1960's the entrance lock was built. Now some of the older docks, no longer needed for present day shipping, have been reclaimed for the Scottish Office building.

The most famous ship built at Leith was the Sirius. She became the first steamship to cross the Atlantic when, during an 18 day voyage, her crew burned wood and resin to keep up steam after the coal ran out! She was built by Menzies and Co. who were the first shipbuilders in Leith. Henry Robb Ltd. who ceased operations in 1984, were the last. Robb's started as a ship repair business in 1918, but gradually absorbed their shipbuilding neighbours like Ramage and Ferguson. They were known for building luxury yachts for the rich and famous. Two of these custom built floating palaces are seen here. The one on the right is unidentified, but the other is the Liberty, just after her launch. She was built in 1907 for an American millionaire, one of three such vessels built in the year. The others were the Hunter and the Lady Blanche.

At the eastern end of Commercial Street is the Custom House, seen here on the right. It was built to replace the old Custom House in Tolbooth Wynd, in 1812 and is now used as a museum store. Beside it was the Lower Drawbridge or Bernard Street Bridge which had large hoop like gantries added to it to carry the electric tram cables so that the bridge could still swing open for passing ships. A range of early nineteenth century bonded warehouses dominates the north side of Commercial Street, opposite them, beside the old Free Church building on the corner of Dock Street is the last remnant of the Citadel, built in 1650 for Oliver Cromwell's army and abandoned ten years later. The North British (later L.N.E.R.) Railway's nearby Citadel Station was occupied for longer and is now used as a youth centre.

BERNARD STREET, LEITH.

When Bernard Street replaced the old Weigh-house Wynd in the late eighteenth century one of the most remarkable urban spaces in Scotland was created. The narrow street that leaves the Shore gives little indication of the wide open space, redolent of country town market squares or Italian piazzas, that it becomes. The finest of its Georgian buildings is the small domed building to the right of the tram here. It was originally the Leith Bank and it's elegance is enhanced by narrow streets on either side which isolate it from other buildings. It is now used by the Portuguese and Australian Consulates. The statue to Rabbie Burns was erected in 1898 by the Leith Burns' Appreciation Society. It makes no mention of the poet's illegitimate daughter Betty, who was born in Leith. Perhaps the Society didn't appreciate that!

Burns' Monument, Corn Exchange and Assembly Rooms, Leith.

Like Bernard Street, Constitution Street was laid out at the end of the eighteenth century. It ran along the line of one of the old ramparts of the 1560 fortifications, cutting off part of the South Leith Parish Church yard in the process. The domed building on the right, partly obscured by the Exchange Buildings, is the Corn Exchange, on the corner with Baltic Street. The Exchange Buildings were built in 1809 and incorporated the old Assembly Rooms. They were the centre of old Leith's social scene while the Exchange buildings and Bernard Street were regarded as the commercial centre. The first tram route in Leith ran from Bernard Street, up Constitution Street to Princes Street in Edinburgh. The same route taken by a team of horses towing the great cannon Mons Meg when it was returned to Scotland in 1829.

The Municipal Buildings and Council Chambers were built five years before Leith became an independent burgh in 1833, but they became a symbol of that independence as Leith struggled to remain separate from Edinburgh. The building is on the corner of Constitution Street and Queen Charlotte Street; originally called Charlotte Street, but as if to rub salt into the wound, the name was changed after amalgamation to avoid confusion with Edinburgh's Charlotte Street! The Leith Police, famous for being able to '...dismisseth us' have used the building since it was erected and it is still used as the D Divisional Headquarters of Lothian and Borders Police. St, John's Church, on the left, with the distinctive octagonal tower, has been converted into offices.

The Scottish Co-operative Wholesale Society set up its second distribution depot in Leith, in 1877. Leith was well placed for the import of grain and dairy produce from Europe and the depot quickly proved to be a success. After only three years it moved into larger, permanent premises in Links Place and Poplar Lane, handling groceries, fruit and vegetables, ham curing, tea and coffee blending and many other items. It even handled cattle sales for a time. Later there was a preserve factory in Bath Street beside the transport garage where this lorry would have been based. It is pictured here beside the Links; a more photogenic location than Bath Street which was re-named Salamander Place, presumably to avoid confusion with Bath Street, Portobello.

The original Seafield tram terminus was in Seafield Place at its junction with Calamander Street and Seafield Road. The tracks were later extended to Portobello. The board in the tram window advertises its route as Stanley Road via Pilrig Street, before that it would have gone along the south side of the Links and Duke Street to Leith Walk, turned into Pilrig Street and run along Newhaven Road to Stanley Road. Leith had covered trams from the beginning of its electric service, this one is helping to exhort people to do their bit for King and Country during the First World War, while the soldiers beside it no doubt regarded the dangers of having a fag as significantly less than a visit to the trenches! The austere warehouse building in the background is part of the Seafield Maltings of Thomas Bernard and Co Ltd.

LEITH LINKS AND ARTHUR'S SEAT, LEITH. (6)   221039. JV

Leith can fairly claim to be the home of golf - eat your heart out Saint Andrews! The earliest record of the game is a ban imposed by King James II in 1457 because it disrupted his army's archery practice on Leith Links. More significantly the rules that formed the basis of the modern game, were written down by Leith's Honourable Company of Edinburgh Golfers in 1744. The Company had a five hole course around the perimeter of the Links, but with many other people using the Links the cry of fore! must have been heard rather too often because they left and now play at the more exclusive surroundings of Muirfield. Other sports like football, cricket and even cock fighting used the links at some time and they were also used for grazing animals and hanging out washing. Originally, when the links extended to the shore, the sands were used for the Leith Races. They too have moved; to Musselburgh.

Restalrig Road runs south from the Links to what was once the small village of Restalrig. The name comes from a family called de Lestalric who settled in the area after the Norman conquest. At the time, Leith was a small village on their lands. The first position taken up by the besieging English army in 1560 appears to have been between Restalrig Road and Lochend Road, where they built a siege fort. It would have taken advantage of the high ground above where Restalrig Terrace is now and it was apparently from here that the guns bombarded the town and damaged Saint Mary's Church and not from mounds on the Links popularly believed to have been siege gun emplacements. It was also from here that siege trenches were dug west towards Pilrig and the Water of Leith.

These buildings near the northern end of Lochend Road have all been replaced by modern flats. Facing the northern end of the road was Leith Academy Secondary School, now used by Queen Margaret College. The original Academy building on the edge of the links replaced the Leith High School in 1898 and later became the Academy's Primary School. It is now, simply, Leith Primary School. In sharp contrast to the blue blazered Academy pupils were the less fortunate boys who found themselves at the Lochend Road Industrial School. But the school became famous for its brass band and their concerts on the Links were apparently much enjoyed by Victorian and Edwardian Leithers. The school is now the Lochend Campus of Telford College.

From the mid sixteenth century timber was stacked and sold at a riverside market on a site now known the Timber Bush; a Leithisation of the French 'bourse' and a reminder of the strong historical French influence in the port. Pit props for the Midlothian mines and soft and hard woods from the Baltic and the Americas were always one of the principal imports through Leith and timber yards spread elsewhere from those early beginnings. Park, Dobson and Co. Ltd's. Eastern Sawmills in Easter Road was one of these. It was situated between the old Caledonian (later L.M.S.) Railway to the right in this picture and the North British (L.N.E.R.) Railway to Leith Central. There were allotments between it and Lochend Road in the top left of the picture.

Sacred to the Memory of THE LEITH HORSE CAR, which has succumbed to Electric Traction.

Entered at Stationers' Hall.   J. Naylor & Co., Leith.

The horse drawn buses which ran from Bernard Street to Princes Street were superseded in 1871 by trams which terminated at Haymarket. Each tram held up to 40 passengers and two horses were needed to pull it, but it was a hard life for a horse and most lasted only about four years. When the operator's franchise expired in 1892 Edinburgh City Corporation took over the portion of the system in the city but the Leith portion remained in private hands, as the Leith Tramway Company. The Burgh finally bought the Leith system in 1903 and put in hand plans to electrify it. This picture postcard, published in the last week of the horse trams, shows one of them passing the printers and stationers Duff and Thomson at 107 -109 Constitution Street.

When Edinburgh took over the trams in the City they were anxious to dispense with horses in favour of a newer technology and set about installing cable cars on Leith Walk. The Burgh, however, wanted a more advanced system and refused to extend the cable to the foot of the Walk, even when the new cars were introduced in 1899. The first electric tram ran on 18th August 1905, just in time for the opening of the Leith Flower Show in Victoria Park. It was a race against time to get the route from the foot of the Walk to Stanley Road ready in time for the show, but, with much relief, it was approved by the Board of Trade inspector a week before the show. The official opening was held in November when the whole system was completed.

221045. J.V.

LEITH WALK LEITH. (12)

With two different systems, the trams of both City and Burgh had to stop at Pilrig and passengers had to change from one to the other, a farcical situation which became known as the 'Pilrig Muddle'. Leith's electric trams were far superior to Edinburgh's cable cars and Leith folk delighted in saying to people going up to Edinburgh; "... if you're in a hurry get off at Pilrig and walk!" Leith shopkeepers too, happily exploited the 'muddle' by advertising it as something people could avoid if they used local shops. The 'muddle' continued until the whole system was electrified after the amalgamation of Leith and Edinburgh. This picture from 1933 shows the benefit as one of the new Edinburgh trams heads past Dalmeny Street and Pilrig unimpeded.

32

THE CROSS, FOOT OF LEITH WALK, LEITH. (13)

While the civic authorities squabbled over the relative merits of tramway systems, the North British (later L.N.E.R.) Railway moved quickly to build a line from Edinburgh Waverley to a huge new station at the foot of Leith Walk called Leith Central. It was opened in 1903. The five minute journey known as the 'penny jump', was an instant success, but after the tram systems were standardised in the 1920's passenger traffic quickly declined and was abandoned after World War 2. Here two Edinburgh trams pass the range of two storey station buildings, in the centre of this 1933 picture. The station site is now a supermarket and leisure facility, but the buildings, including the distinctive clock tower at the corner of Leith Walk and Duke Street, survive.

Like Constitution Street, Great Junction Street runs along the line of one of the ramparts of the great 1560 defences. It was laid out in 1818 and is now a mixture of tenements and smaller buildings. The shop on the ground floor of this distinctive block on the corner with Kirkgate appears always to have been a shoe shop, but the street still retains the wide variety of shops, that was once the hallmark of the Kirkgate. It also includes the bonded warehouses of John Crabbie & Co. Ltd., makers of Green Ginger Wine, Dr. Bell's school (Doc'y Bell's) and at the west end, Leith Hospital. Next to the hospital was the Eldorado stadium in Mill Lane. Wrestlers at the Eldorado never seemed to get hurt, but staff at the hospital apparently remember attending to numerous injuries when the stadium was used by skateboarders in the 1970's.

Junction Street Leith

The hospital was just beyond the turreted building in the centre of this view which was built in 1911 for the Leith Provident Co-operative Society Ltd. The Society had opened its first shop in 1878 in Great Junction Street and 'the store' as it was known locally was always a feature of the street. In the 1960's, the Co-op built a supermarket and 'furnishing emporium' on the site of the St. James, Episcopal Hall, on the right. A plaque on the adjacent building declares it as the site of the birthplace of Sir John Gladstone, father of the Liberal Prime Minister William Ewart Gladstone. Leith was, until the rise of the Labour Party, a Liberal stronghold and such was the pride in their Prime Ministerial connections that Leith Liberals campaigned for Parliament as Gladstonian candidates!

Over two hundred soldiers from the 7th Royal Scots, Leith's Territorial Army battalion were killed in Britain's worst railway disaster on 22nd May 1915. The crash, at Quintinshill near Gretna on the Scottish border, occurred when an error by a signalman led to the troop train colliding with a stationary train. Seconds later a London to Glasgow express ploughed into the wreckage. Of 486 officers and men, 418 were killed or injured in the crash and ensuing fire; an appalling disaster, even by First World War standards. It took three hours for this funeral procession, seen here in Pilrig Street, to go from the drill hall in Dalmeny Street to Rosebank Cemetery. A memorial has been erected there to these young men who gave their lives for their country as surely as if they had carried on to die on the bloody sands of Gallipoli.

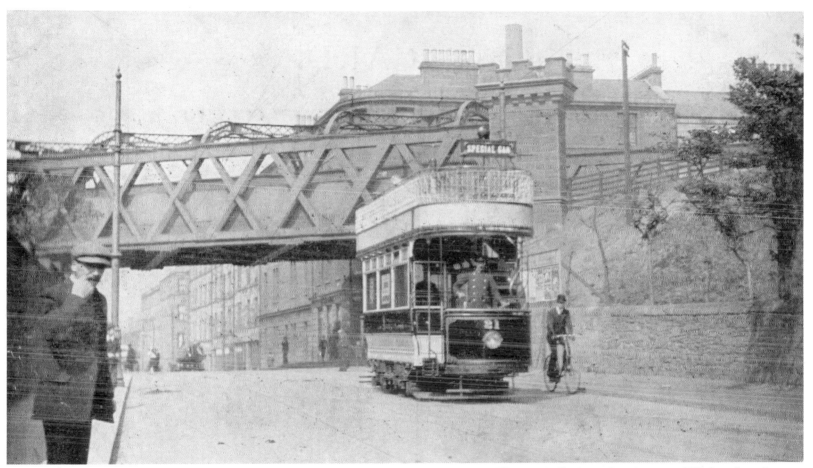

Rosebank Cemetery is out of picture on the left of this view of the Bonnington, or Pilrig Toll. The boundary between Edinburgh and Leith ran along Pilrig Street and Newhaven Road and the toll was at their junction with Bonnington Road. The Old Toll Bar, in the distinctive tenement behind the tram, is a reminder of old divisions. The lattice girder bridge between tram and tenement carried the Caledonian (later L.M.S.) Railway's Leith Branch diagonally across the road junction. Less than half a mile on the Edinburgh side of Bonnington Toll is the Powderhall stadium, one time home of the New Year sprint and in the 1920's home ground of Leith's senior football team Leith Athletic, one of seven grounds they occupied in their sixty seven year history. They were second division champions three times, but went into liquidation in 1954.

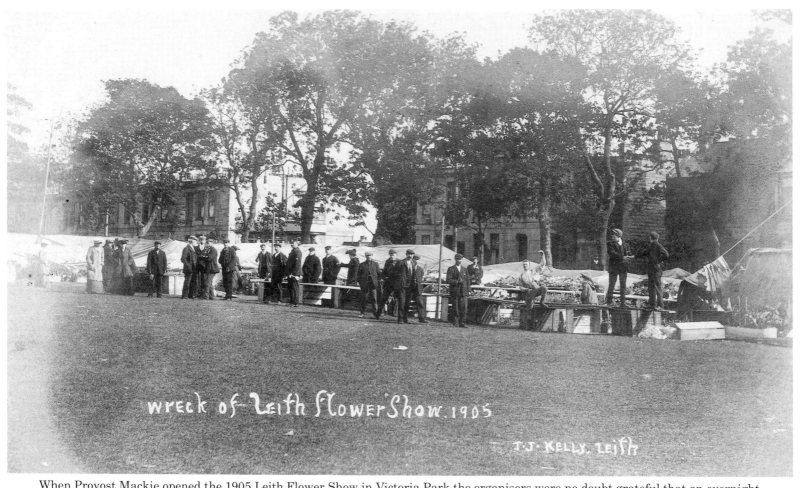

wreck of Leith Flower Show. 1905

J.J. KELLY. Leith

When Provost Mackie opened the 1905 Leith Flower Show in Victoria Park the organisers were no doubt grateful that an overnight storm had given way to sunshine, but just before seven the following morning another storm blew up. Wind and rain battered the site. The 220feet x 40feet marquee was lifted off the ground; the heavy poles and soaking canvas crashed down on the exhibits inside. Plants and crochet work alike were ruined. But it's an ill wind that doesn't blow somebody some good and T Johnstone Kelly, a photographer from Ferry Road, was quickly on the spot and by mid-morning had produced this and other picture postcards, for which there was apparently a steady demand. Despite the disaster, the sports, always the principal attraction of the second day of the show, were only slightly delayed.

38

NEWHAVEN ROAD, LEITH.

Crowds, encouraged by the start of the new tram service, converged on the park in great numbers and the entertainments, illuminated by electric arc lamps (!), continued until 11.00 pm. Tickets were sold at booths in Newhaven Road, to avoid a bottleneck at the park gates. But not everyone was pleased. One man wrote to the local paper objecting to the park being used for a '... third rate Waverley Market carnival'. Sadly for him the Show returned the following year, but the Leith Horticultural, Industrial and Sports Society Ltd. who ran the show, got into financial difficulties after the 1912 Show bringing it all to an end. One memory remains in the park, a small fountain near the bowling greens was presented to the Burgh by the Society in 1899.

Ferry Road, Leith.

Ferry Road was built up in the nineteenth century with mainly middle class housing replacing hitherto undeveloped countryside. It runs almost straight for three miles to its junction here with North Junction Street. Just out of picture on the left, is where the Town Hall and Library were built in 1929. The Town Hall, and the David Kilpatrick School behind it, were bombed during the Second World War. The Town Hall was re-built in the 1960's. At one time there was a dentist in the two storey building on the corner and, as indicated by the sign, there was one in the tenement block on the right too; there is still a dentist there! The tram here is heading along North Junction Street toward Junction Bridge, past the distinctive tenement and a row of small shops on the corner of North Junction Street and Coburg Street. The shops were supported by stilts from the river valley below.

Entrance to Leith Fort

One of the military men who threatened Leith was the Scot, John Paul Jones who commanded the American navy when it appeared off Leith in 1779. He created quite a stir, because the port had no defences and so to guard against any future threat, the Fort was built. It was garrisoned by the Royal Artillery and later accommodated RASC and Pay Corps. It was demolished in the 1950's. The perimeter wall, the entrance gate in North Fort Street and the guard houses were all left standing so that this view of it has not changed much, although the flats that replaced the original Georgian buildings probably look more like barracks than they did! There was Soldier's home in North Fort Street too which provided soldiers with a place to escape to from barracks life.

These tenements in Albany Street and Hamburgh Place have gone, but while Albany Street is now known as Portland Street the name of Hamburgh Place has been retained. Opposite the end of Albany Street was Leith Station, the passenger terminus of the Caledonian (later L.M.S.) Railway - the one that can be seen passing the Eastern Sawmills on page 29 and crossing Bonnington Toll on page 37. From here the railway was extended east into the docks. The nearby junction of Lindsay Road, Commercial Street and North Junction Street was cratered by a wartime bomb. Trams had to stop at the ends of each road in three latter day equivalents of the Pilrig muddle. Further west along Lindsay Road two mountainous tower blocks called Grampian and Cairngorm have swamped the old streets.

George Street, Leith.

A.2600.

George Street was a continuation of North Fort Street, but is now called North Fort Street too. Beyond the end of the street, in this picture from 1935, is a tram crossing the railway bridge in Lindsay Road, while behind it a steamer heads across the Forth. The view of the sea has now been completely obscured by Allied Mills' Chancelot Mill. It was built by the Scottish Co-operative Wholesale Society in the 1960's to replace their original mill in Gosford Place and Dalmeny Road, on ground reclaimed before and during the early years of the Second World War. A bomb dropped in George Street early in the war demolished a tenement next to the garage, just out of picture on the left. At the foot of the street, the extension roof of the Halfway House pub can be seen on the right hand side.

66017

Annfield Promenade, Leith

J.V.

The turreted tenement on the right of this 1909 view is Anchorfield; Annfield Terrace is to the right of it. Annfield was a wonderful place for children. They could run out of the door and across the street to the sea, but on wild winter days it was the sea that ran across the street to Annfield, frequently spraying the houses and on occasions, before proper sea defences were built, washing away the road. But all that changed when this whole area between the Leith west pier and Newhaven Pier was enclosed as the Western Harbour. The work was started in 1936 and continued into the war years using Dutch land reclamation specialists; but the presence of so many foreign workers near wartime installations worried the Admiralty who had them interned until satisfied that the only threat they presented was to the beach.

Newhaven.
New Lane.

Annfield and New Lane here, were regarded as the 'new town' of Newhaven. Like George Street the view across the Forth from New Lane is now blocked by dock buildings, but if you are tall enough you can just see over them to Fife, from where this picture was taken in the 1880's. The view isn't the only thing to have changed, the houses have been replaced by modern replicas; pale shadows of these characterful originals and where the street lamp stood is now a junction box for the fibre optic cables of the information super highway! Between the lane and the sea was Newhaven Links and the area where the fishing cobles were pulled up was known as the Hally. Life in these little houses was not perhaps as picturesque as it looks, domestic waste lay rotting in the gutter in the centre of the lane until it was washed away by the rain.

Newhaven appears to have been a tiny fishing hamlet before King James IV developed it as a Royal harbour and dockyard which he hoped would rival Leith. Here he gave life to his plans for a Scottish navy by building the largest warship of the day, the Great Michael. She was launched in 1511. All the forests of Fife and beyond were felled for her timbers, but a poor nation like Scotland could ill afford such a grand gesture and when James and the Flower of Scotland were killed at the Battle of Flodden, the great ship was sold to France. But soon after the launch James had sold Newhaven to Edinburgh and so when Newhaveners settled back down to the life of a fishing village they did so as free people. Nearly four hundred years later this is what their Main Street looked like; Victoria School dominates the view.

Main Street, Newhaven

Early in the nineteenth century, buildings in Main Street were concentrated on the north side, with closes and wynds running between them to the shore. By the end of the century the south side had been developed too and the spire added to Saint Andrew's Free Church, in the distance. Beside the tram, on the right, is the Peacock Hotel. It was established in 1767 and became famous for sea food. It was also famous for its green piano, when owned by the former Hibs goalkeeper Tommy Younger. On the other side of the street is the foot of Newhaven Road which between here and Jessfield Terrace is known as Whale Brae, for reasons that are now no longer certain. The shop on the corner was Miller's newsagent and hardware store and there were two ice cream shops in the street, Crolla's and Rinaldi's.

The pier was a simple fishing pier at the start of the eighteenth century. Later it became a slipway for ferry services to Fife and a steamer pier was added to the east side. To begin with the fishermen were not allowed to use the new pier because the steamer operators thought that the rough fishermen would upset their passengers, but they got exclusive use of it when Granton harbour was developed in the 1840's and the ferries started to operate from there. The fishermen's lobbying for a proper harbour eventually succeeded when the breakwater was completed in 1878. The fishmarket was added in 1896. It attracted dozens of boats and hundreds of buyers from all over Scotland and continued to function until recently. It is now the site of an excellent museum and a Harry Ramsden's fish and chip restaurant.

Pier Place, Newhaven.

A. 2599.

Pier Place initially went from the Marine Hotel corner to the harbour and fishmarket, but was later extended in front of the Peacock Hotel, Victoria School and the Links. At the end of the east pier, beside the harbour entrance, was the lighthouse. It presented an enduring challenge to generations of local youngsters with a taste for adventure who would run round it, or more accurately, inch fearfully around the narrow ledge with the sea swirling below. The taste of Mason's pies appears equally memorable. Children sent to collect pies for the family often found themselves trotting home with a string handled paper carrying bag full of pies for the neighbours as well. The bakery, just out of the picture on the right, also made vanilla slices that were so good they sold the trimmed edges as 'a bag of cuttings'.

"Four Generations", Newhaven Fishwives.

4.4369. J.V.

The wives of Newhaven fishermen were expected to be able to bait a hook and lug a creel of fish. Marriage outside the village and especially to anyone from Leith was not encouraged and so Newhaven people tended to look quite distinctive. They dressed differently too, particularly the women. Their double skirts were about mid-calf in length and the outer garment was hitched up to provide a cushion for the creel, which could weigh 150 pounds or more. Their plain working clothes contrasted with the more decorative Sunday best. The fishwives cries of Caller Herring or Caller Ou (if they were selling oysters) were among the more famous of Edinburgh's street cries, although they didn't confine their activities to the capital sometimes travelling to places thirty miles away to sell their fish.

NEWHAVEN SILVER PRIZE BAND.

Fishwives choirs were famous too. They have performed on stages to international audiences and their singing tradition still carries on today. The song most closely associated with them is 'Caller herrin'', composed by Lady Nairne to celebrate the herring fishery. Fishermen too have their musical traditions. Apart from the hymn singing that was so important to a seafaring community they used to sing rythmic chanting songs when dredging for oysters. The practical reason was to maintain a constant rowing speed to keep the oyster rake at a constant angle, but there was also a belief that the singing helped to charm the oysters into the nets! The Newhaven Silver Band was also part of the musical tradition of the area before the First World War. It is seen here outside Starbank House.

Starbank Park, Newhaven.

A.2601.

Slum clearances in Victorian towns and cities were often accompanied by the creation of public parks to provide fresh air lungs for the town. Leith was no exception. Victoria Park, where the flower show was wrecked in 1905, was one such park, created out of a private estate, Starbank Park was another. The council bought Starbank House at the end of the nineteenth century and its gardens were landscaped to form the park. The centrepiece is the star shaped flowerbed on the bank in front of Starbank House seen in this view from the 1930's. The House was used as a museum for a while. Just out of the picture on the left is the other main feature of the park, the Devlin Fountain. It was presented in 1910 by local trawler owner and businessman Thomas Devlin.

Starbank Park is in the distance of this view looking east from Trinity Crescent. It is an uncomfortable mixture of Georgian crescent and Victorian tenement; behind it was Trinity railway station on the North British (later L.N.E.R.) Railway that ran along the sea front to Granton. The horse bus is passing the pier house of the old chain pier. The pier was opened in 1821 to provide deep water for the early steamers, which found Leith's tidal restrictions difficult. It was 500 feet long and was like a suspension bridge supported by wooden towers. It was erected just before George IV's visit to Edinburgh, but a proposal that he should use it instead of the traditional royal landing place at Leith, caused an outcry. He landed at Leith! Most steamers stopped using the pier when Granton harbour was opened.

The Chain Pier, Trinity, Edinburgh
destroyed by Storm, Oct. 17, 1898

The pier became a centre for sea bathing when the steamers stopped using it; swimming competitions were held from it and the pavilion at the end was used as a gymnasium, but the flimsy looking structure couldn't withstand one of the worst storms to hit the east coast of Scotland. It started on Sunday 15th October 1898 and by the time it began to abate four days later it had done terrible damage all along the coast. The half of the pier nearest the road had collapsed by early afternoon on the Tuesday and the rest was swamped by the rising tide, only the central support and the bathing station at the end were left visible. Even the pub, in the pier house at the road end, was in danger of being dragged into the sea. It survived, but the damage to the pier was estimated at £500 and it was never re-built.

There were many casualties at sea. The steamer Paola of West Hartlepool foundered on Pallas Rock. Her crew were rescued by a Newhaven pilot boat before she went down. The Norwegian barque Kawa sought shelter in the Forth, but lost her anchor off Gullane and was driven ashore at Annfield. The schooner Ida was towed into Granton after a Russian barque had crashed into her. Three ships were wrecked at Cramond and another went ashore near Queensferry. Their stranded crews filled the Sailor's Home in Leith to bursting point, but one crew that didn't have to go there were from James Currie and Co's Buda. Her skipper misread navigation lights and she ended up on the beach at Montrose instead of alongside in her home port of Leith.

BIBLIOGRAPHY

Ian Brodie	Steamers of the Forth: David and Charles 1976
John Thomas	Gretna, Britain's Worst Railway Disaster (1915): David and Charles 1969
Leith Local History Project	Leith Lives, a series of booklets, various titles: 1980's.
Tom McGowran	Newhaven-on-Forth, Port of Grace: John Donald 1985.
James Scott Marshall	The Life and Times of Leith: John Donald 1985.
Joyce Wallace	Traditions of Trinity and Leith: John Donald 1985.
Joyce Wallace	Further Traditions of trinity and Leith: John Donald 1990.
Sue Mowatt	The Port of Leith: John Donald and Forth Ports PLC 1994.
James Kinloch and John Butt	History of the Scottish Co-operative Wholesale Society Ltd.: S.C.W.S. 1981.
Stuart Harris	The Fortifications and Siege of Leith, a paper in the Proceedings of the Society of Antiquaries of Scotland 1991.
Brian J Hunter	The Defunct Soccer Clubs of Edinburgh: Daniel Stewart's College, library project 1969.
David H A Boyd	Leith Hospital 1848-1988: Scottish Academic Press 1990

ACKNOWLEDGEMENTS

It must be the height of impudence for someone from Glasgow to write a book about Edinburgh, but Leith is different and has in some respects more in common with the great city of the west than the city it is now part of. But my connections are better than that. My wife was born in Leith and grew up in Trinity, her grandfather opposed amalgamation with Edinburgh. His daughter, my mother-in-law, Becky Welsh was a great help telling me about her early life; what she says about the New 'Kir'gate' couldn't be printed! Thanks Becky! And thanks too to sister-in-law, Joan.

The staff at Lamb's House were very helpful, I enjoyed sitting in on a reminiscence group there and am grateful to the people there for allowing me to listen to their memories. The Leith Library is what a local library should be, full of local material that I could consult 'on location' rather than having to separate research on the ground from book work - great! The staff at the new Newhaven Museum were very helpful and the displays excellent and informative.

Margaret Graham was a great help with historical anecdote and the supply of pictures on pages 4, 14, 24, 25, 36, 43,46, 49, 51, 52 and the back cover. I am very grateful too to George Waugh who supplied the pictures on the title page and pages 2, 7, 15,18,22, 23, 30, 37,39, 45, 47 and the inside back cover. Thanks too to Anthony Duda for the picture on page 29.